LITERARY LIFE

LITERARY LIFE

Posy Simmonds

JONATHAN CAPE
LONDON

Published by Jonathan Cape 2003

8 10 9

Copyright © Posy Simmonds 2003

Posy Simmonds has asserted her right under the Copyright, Designs
and Patents Act 1988 to be identified as the author of this work

First published in cartoon strip form in the *Guardian*

First published in book form in Great Britain in 2003 by
Jonathan Cape
Random House, 20 Vauxhall Bridge Road,
London SW1V 2SA

Random House Australia (Pty) Limited
20 Alfred Street, Milsons Point, Sydney,
New South Wales 2061, Australia

Random House New Zealand Limited
18 Poland Road, Glenfield,
Auckland 10, New Zealand

Random House South Africa (Pty) Limited
Endulini, 5A Jubilee Road, Parktown 2193, South Africa

The Random House Group Limited Reg. No. 954009

A CIP catalogue record for this book
is available from the British Library

ISBN 978-0-224-07269-4

Papers used by The Random House Group Limited are natural,
recyclable products made from wood grown in sustainable forests;
the manufacturing processes conform to the environmental
regulations of the country of origin

Printed and bound in India by
Replika Press Pvt. Ltd.

LITERARY LIFE

Rustic Block

9.05am

Chapter One: It was raining. The sheep were

9.20am

It was raining. The sheep were in the field.

10.15am

It was pouring. The sheep languished in the field. The gutters dripped. The clock ticked.

10.50am

Hannah yawned, "Wish I'd never moved to the country. You feel positively catatonic. You can't think of any

11.45am

"Christ", snarled Hannah. "Wish to hell I'd never moved to effing, sodding Suffolk. Had a brain once. In Kentish Town I used to

12.30pm

Suddenly one of the Jacob ewes ran amok, stabbing, slashing and gouging a bloody path as it

Bastards!

Bastards!

I TOLD you, Penny!

I KNEW this'd happen!

What? What's happened, sweetums?

Boulder Books! For godsake, that's what! It's their first day open...or hadn't you noticed?

We've had precisely THREE customers all morning....Down the road they're bloody seething with 'em!

Well, it's a huge new shop, ducky... People are curious..

That's not curiosity—that's the shape of things to come! Kiss of Death for this shop, I'm telling you!

These bloody Mega stores!

Make my blood boil!

They sniff a good spot. Muscle in. Slash, discount ...undercut everybody... Then they hoover up all the local custom....

And if you're a small, independent bookseller and you go to the wall.... well, tough sh*t!

God I HATE Boulder Books!

Bloody Boulder Books!

Leeches!

Hyenas!

Bastards

Colin, dear heart... Would you just shut up and come inside?

..only you're driving all the customers away

Bastards

Time goes by...

CANOVA BOOKS
LAUNCH PARTY FOR
EMMA TOGEL
PALMERSTON ROOM

Hiii

Can we have your name, please?

It's weird...You know, for years 'n' years, whenever I saw something *leggy*, in black, like that....

...I'd think: *Hot Patootie!*... and imagine them pleasuring my body.

Scary thing is...

...now I think: oh, it's just one of the publicity department ...and only imagine them flogging my novel...

Right... anyone else have a question for our panel of distinguished authors?

Er, yeah...I'd like to ask **Dan Rutland**....

..er, the theme of all your books is a society gone **totely** down the tubes...er...

...er, full of every sort of degradation and stuff, you know, like massive **drug abuse**...

...weird sex... ..murder...

Rape...incest...

...extreme violence.. ..er..**sadism**...

..alchoholism...**coprophilia**... etcetera, etcetera...er... All described in highly convincing and, well, **horrific** detail...er...

What I'd like to ask Dan is: Where d'you get your ideas?....

..And are any of them based on your own personal experience?

So, Dan... over to you

Golly.. that's a tricky one... Well..it's all my imagination, really..I mmm...

"...but see, they aren't really them...they've
just changed into them, 'cos they took the magic
Polyjuice potion...so Harry becomes Crabbe, Ron becomes Goyle...
Hermione becomes Millicent Bulstrode, who's like in Slytherin House.
Not in Griffender House, like Harry....and so, well, anyway, remember
I said the Hogwarts caretaker has this cat with bulgy eyes,
called Mrs Norris? Well, she was like found petrified in a passage...
So was Colin Creevy. And so then Harry decommmm lhmllmllnmllllllm...
mmn mmmmlmlln lmmmlmmmllm "

The rep from Dyna-Globe makes his monthly call...

Gilly and I moved to the country three years ago...

Almost immediately, we joined the local Reading Group, which now holds its weekly meetings at _our_ house...

...partly because we are conveniently placed, but mainly, I suspect, because Gilly is lavish with the booze. She's _obsessed_ with this bloody group..It's **HELL**!

I'm getting so **fed up** - she talks to them more than me!

Gilly gets so much out of these evenings with Mia, Sally, Tamsin, May, Teresa, Pauline and Roger Tupper..

...I think you have a point, Roger...

But should we be judging Captain Corelli by these criteria?

Whereas all **I** get is endless bollockings:...for smoking...for yawning...for talking...

...for falling asleep...for being assertive... for _not_ being assertive.

Cli-ive! How many times? The rules are: you must address **THE GROUP**! No tête à têtes with Mia!

Z Z Z Z

Oh God! Honestly, Clive!

Well, so bloody **WHAT**, if we're **safe** and middle-brow?!! Look, smartarse, we haven't all got university degrees! **We're** not trying to be **clever**! We're extending our range at our own pace!

Clive, can you just stop **agreeing** like that with everybody? You don't mean it.... and, anyway, we're not interested in con-sensus...

To be frank, I suppose it's a way of getting my wife's attention...

No, sorry, I can't bring myself to read **ANY** of these books

God! You're such a **SNOB**, Clive!

Actually, to be completely frank, I've just had a major row with that bastard, Roger Tupper.

He's had it in for me all along...

Male jealousy - he can't _stand_ my encroaching on his literary harem...

HOW **DARE** YOU!!!

So. I've exiled myself from the Reading Group. Banished myself from my own sitting-room. They are all still in there... but, what's for sure, they're not discussing the Campus Novel...

SUGA

NAUSEA

ALBERT CAMUS **THE OUTSIDER**

They're discussing **ME**!

*Would you just imagine, for one moment the **HORROR** of this?....*

OWEN LLOYD
WILL SIGN COPIES OF HIS NEW NOVEL "BREATH" 3.30-4.30pm

*...Just **imagine** the sheer gut-wrenching, butt-clenching, unspeakable **VILENESS** of being ignored by the general public.....*

...this is an announcement for customers... Author Owen Lloyd is currently signing copies of his new.....

poetry

fiction

IMAGINE *having to endure this soul-crushing humiliation!* **IMAGINE** *chewing the bitter cud of rejection!*

IMAGINE *having to abide the lame protestations of the shop personnel...or the stony concern of Debra, the girl from my publishers....*

Yeah... it's funny - there were masses of people here lunch time... Must be the rain... Could be the pre-season lull, of course...

..or the football

...But, I mean, last week, when Jackie was here...it was crazy! Queue went out of the door!

*And then imagine the **AGONY** of spotting one of my enemies on his way upstairs to the café.... from where he observes at leisure my failure to sell a **single** copy.*

Hi, Owen!

It's **HELL**, I tell you!

OK Owen, I think we could call it a day...

People just have **no** idea what writers go through! They've no idea what it's like to sit...inwardly begging someone - **ANYONE!** - to stop and part with some cash...

OWEN LLOYD

People just don't realise what it's like...to be ignored ....

...to be treated with callous indifference... It's **hell**, I tell you!

Animals
Biography
Café
Fiction
Gardening

BOOKS

Any spare change, please

I'll call you a cab

POPPY!

Knock! Knock!

Ohno! We've overslept!
...It's my DAD!....
..oh..and my mum!

✱♪✱!! They're not going to come in, are they?!

O God...Mum's O.K....but my Dad won't like you being here....

Poppy!...Poppy? D'you know what time it is?.....

It's lunch time

Poppy? You still in bed?

Whatever time did you get in?

Poppy! Answer us, please...

Poppy, have you forgotten your homework?

I know you've got a lot.

Staying out so late isn't any way to get your A Levels, you know...

Have you done your English?...... Poppy, are you going to open the door?

Oh, Poppy! God you look rough

Hi Mum! Hi Dad!

Yes, I know I do!

See,... My heart aches, and a drowsy numbness..pains... My sense, as though of hemlock I had drunk... erm...

...something.. Dance and Provencal song and Sunburnt mirth...O for a beaker full of the warm South..

Full of the true, the blushful Hippocrene!

...with beaded bubbles winking at the brim!

overdid the Old Hippocrene, last night, did you?

Still, you've been a good girl doing your English!

Well, that's excellent! She's been learning the Romantics

"You know, you're really beautiful.... Have you ever thought of being a novelist?"

...You just don't know **HOW** I long to be left alone...

Yeah Yeah

...I mean, at the moment, it's totally ✳✳✳ing crazy! It's **relentless** the publicity I've had to do!...**four** interviews Friday...TV crew in my house whole of Saturday...**two** signings...**Front Row**, Channel 4 today! **I'm DEAD!** I'm wiped out! I'm...

Yeah, well you could always say **NO**, Sean...

But it's like everyone **HAS** to have a piece of **ME**! God, I'm like just **SO-O-O** tired of jumping through media hoops! I mean, I'm a **writer**, not a ✳✳✳✳ing **performer**....but people just don't get it — they keep wanting **me** to do stuff...

Like I said... You could always say no to them.

You feel so **NAKED**! I can't go anywhere, now, without being recognised....like, **see what I mean** — those two, over there...

You can't imagine what it's like having women stare at you... having them proposition you all the time....

No, I'm sure I can't, Sean... Tell me about it

You wait...any minute now they'll be over: "Excuse me, you're Sean Poker, aren't you? I just love your books blablabla..."... Price one pays, I suppose...but, God, it gets **BORING**! People just **WON'T** let you alone.

›SIGH!‹

Well, tell them to ✳✳✳✳ off, then! Ever tried that!?

Not...in so many words. No.

What about violence? Tried that? Hitting people. Or stabbing them. They'd soon learn to avoid you....

Ssh! They're getting up! Don't **LOOK**! They're coming over!

What're they doing? What're they doing?

They're leaving.

They've left you alone.

Bitches

Linda, hi... yeah, I'm good...listen, you know that bloke I met the other night...?

Advertising bloke, that's right... art director at Nagel Sweetman....

...yeah, well he's just sent me some *underwear*...

Underwear!?

—Yeah!

Pants.. **Alvin Lorenzo** ones...white cotton... yeah, they're not bad...

Anyway, **Nagel**-thingy do all the **Alvin Lorenzo** ads... ..and this guy says they're having this big, new campaign...**AND WOULD I** like to think about modelling the pants and stuff?!!

Sean! NO!! What??

No, **really!** He said I'd be **perfect** because I've got that extra dimension...

'cos I'm a writer, not just a pretty face har har!

But, you know, they want this sort of **I.Q** plus muscles plus culture...conflation..... It's a massive campaign—he's talking **mega** posters..super sites

And you know, I thought, God, I could be really **UP THERE**!...

But then I thought, frankly, is this the sort of exposure I want....?

I mean, you know, you have to ask yourself... Would Rushdie do it? Would Garcia Marquez? ...McEwan? Hornby?

Would Dickens have done it?

Tolstoy..?

It was only then we noticed Captain Tozer standing at the bottom of the firestep.

"I so disagree with you... How *naif* you are," he drawled. "D'you really believe anything can **prevent** a war, once the politicians get keen on the idea?"

"I mean, it would be like trying to cancel one of my dear *mother's* balls. Once enough preparations have been made, the date fixed, invitations sent, there's NO turning back. It has to take place. Exactly the same with war."

A few yards down the line, our trench mortars hurled a short-range barrage into the wood.
Afterwards, the same eerie silence fell. Captain Tozer mounted the firestep and peered cautiously over the top.

"Y'know, I think Fritz has abandoned his forward trenches." He turned and gave me a cold look.

"Jackson, you and Private Fielding, go and take a squint."
We made a low, darting scramble up the shell-pocked slope. The enemy, if they were there, continued to hold their fire. Quite soon I was panting by the smashed parapet of what seemed to be a deserted trench.

There was nobody in the dugout either. But there were signs of a hasty retreat: candles smouldering on a table, the remains of a meal – bacon, rye bread, schnapps.

"Blimey, this is paradise," whispered Fielding.
"Look at the luxury!" He kicked a battered armchair whose stuffing...

Yes, it was in all the broadsheets on Thursday...
...and I...I was the facilitator, if you like....

I mean, I organised it because everyone I'd met lately seemed to feel the same...you know, this sense of DREAD........
...*creative paralysis*...This sort of horrible, creeping bunker mentality...

And so I thought a letter to the papers — a "we, the undersigned" sort of thing. I mean, no bloody use *really* ...just a register of protest. But at least something we could do as *writers*...*poets*...*authors*, famous or otherwise

...and I thought...a strong, well-argued, anti-war statement...lots of signatories, great and small... Well, you know, it just might produce some sort of reaction...

And has it?

Tsk, well, you didn't ask ME!

Too early to tell **REALLY**... But there has been an initial reaction — the usual, predictable, knee-jerk stuff, you know, like...

...like "If so and so got their name *printed*, why wasn't *mine*?"

..Yeah, me too! Why were our names lumped in afterwards with "**and others**"?

...Oh, God, **Zoë**...I ask myself...**WHY** are we open today?

16 WINTERGREENES 16
BOOKS

Ghastly, bloody time of year! No customers, except those you want to kill.....

≥ *SOTTO VOCE* ≥
I mean, look at **that!** **REALLY!** Tsk..dripping all over the books!

Excuse me, shall I put your umbrella over by the door for you?

What?

No s'OK

You happy browsing? Or d'you need any help?....

No. Just looking

"Just looking" till it stops raining...

utter worm cast!

≥ *Aa-tishoo!*

BOOK EVENTS

≥ *Aachooo* ≥

Oh GREAT! Thanks! **DO** sneeze over everything...and **do** wipe your snot on the new novels.... **Lovely!** Thank you so much, you....

D'you need a tissue, Sir?

What?

NO

And you're sure you're happy browsing?

YES!

I am

Barbarian! That's right, crack the spines, crease all the covers! **Thank you so much!**

No! Zoë, would you believe it!? Now he's **EATING!!!** God! Chocolate thumb-prints everywhere! And there goes the wrapper on the floor!

The dirty sod!

Excuse me, sir...you just dropped some-thing......

Oh fer Godsake!

Have you got nothing better to do!?

Nothing better to do?

..no, I don't think so....

...But tell me the author and we'll order it for you!

"...and when, you know, any minute we could all die of smallpox..or anthrax, ...you think 'Why? **Why** does one *write*? What a futile occupation! What difference could a bloody book make to anything!?'..... and then you think ' No, come on... isn't that something rather magnificent — sitting at one's P.C. in the face of Armageddon?' And that, in a nutshell, is the theme of my ....."

"... yes, yes... I know that, Rebecca, I **know** times change.. yes, okay
point taken, it's **not** my business... but, Rebecca, **someone's** got to say
this: **Wh**y have we sunk to this? **Why're** we publishing this **disgusting** book? What?.. But I don't give
a toss if it's brilliant! Just look at it! Look at the ✳✳✳ing awful binding... endpapers 're much too thin!
Look how far the bloody cover boards overhang! And all that **glue**! No wonder the book won't stay open
~which it won't anyway, because the ✳✳✳ing grain of the paper goes the wrong ✳✳✳ing way! And the
setting! Who can read a line that long?....and all these paragraphs beginning on the last line of the page!
And as for all the ✳✳✳ing **literals**!... What? I keep telling you, I don't care if it's brilliant...it's a bloody..."

Ecstasy

We found an estimated **670** matching books on our database for author: Owen **LLOYD**

2. Owen **LLOYD** — **Heavy Water**. Gulland Press, 1979. First edition. scarce firs... 213 pages. Good copy of author's novel. Covers slightly dusty. Price: U.S. $ **204.70**. Bookseller: K.P. Rare Books — London, U.K.

Ooh... $204 for my first little book

3. Owen **LLOYD** — **The Matchwood Diary**. Gulland Press, 1981. First edition. Signed by the author. Small stain to top edge. Minor creasing to bottom of wrapper. Good copy. Price: U.S. $ **375.00**. Bookseller: Coyne. New Y... USA

Ooh better!

4. Owen **LLOYD** — **The Matchwood Diary**. Gulland Press 1981. First edition. Very nice copy in near fine dustwrapper. Just a few spots of foxing to bottom and fore edge. Price: U.S. $ **520.00**. Bookseller: Bibliophone, De... MI, USA

...wha-hey! 520 dollars!

5. Owen **LLOYD** **Morwenna** — Crichton & Duff 1984 First edition. 30 poems in 3 parts. One of 400 numbered copies signed by the author. Covers lightly dust-soiled. Otherwise, good copy. Price: U.S. $ **778·52** Armitage Rare Books Poole UK

$778! Wow! My god!

Cri-key!

6. Owen **LLOYD** **Morwenna** — Crichton and Duff 1984 First edition. One of 400 numbered copies signed by the author on the front free endpaper. Cover- one small [1 cm] scratch in the laminate on the spine. Very good copy. Price: U.S. $ **790·00** Bookseller: ABD Toronto, Ont. Canada

God!!! Even better!

Terrific!

7. Owen **LLOYD** **Morwenna** — Crichton & Duff 1984. First edition. One of 400 numbered copies. Inscribed in Welsh by the author on the first blank:
* "Anwylaf, Teresa, seren fy mywyd, gan gofio Fenis, Owen."

!!

* Dearest Teresa, Star of my life Remembering Venice

Agony

My God, Teresa! How **could** you!? How **could** you, you **treacherous** **bitch**!?...it was my parting gift! **I** still treasure **yours**! How **could** you do this?! How could you **sell** it ...you unfeeling, **callous**, bloody b\.....

P.L.

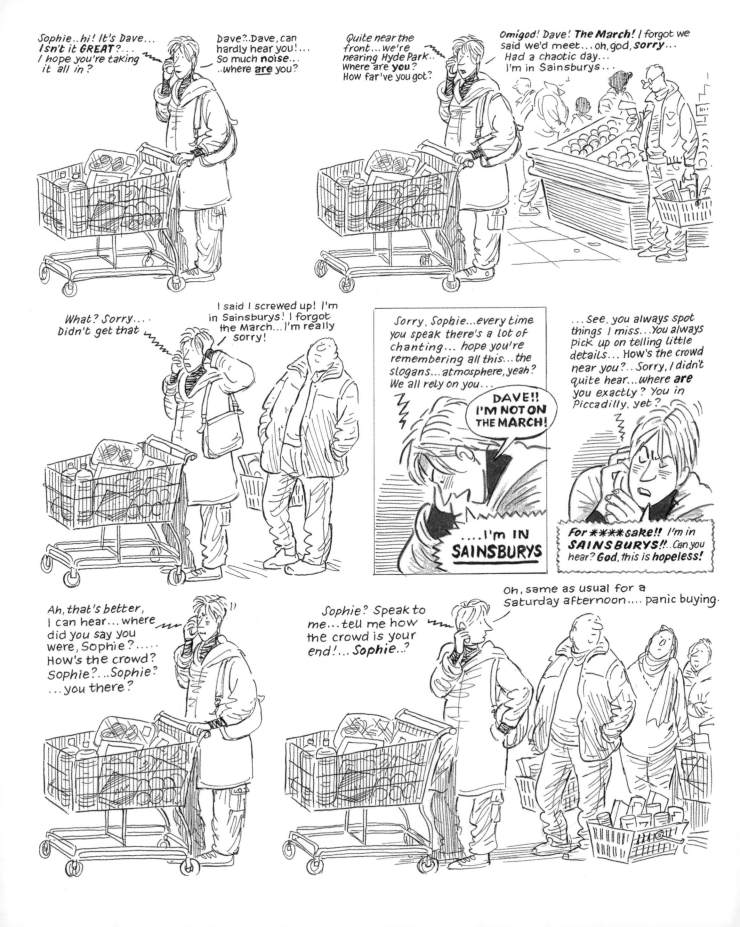

SUCCESS

It's for Sally and Ben.. Thanks!

Thank **YOU!**

Hi

Would you like it signed for anyone particular?

ur..yeah.. for **Ian**.. cheers

I like your stuff!

Just your name and the date...

Ur...you ever think of writing anything really **serious**? ....

Hal-lo! We're **such** fans! We've brought **ALL** our old copies of your books...you wouldn't mind signing them too, would you?

God!! £16·99!

Just for a load of **blokesy**, middle-class **crap!**

Excuse me, you don't know if there's a toilet on this floor, do you?

No sorry.

Could you write **Happy birthday**, too? Thank you so much...

Thank **YOU!**

Uh...I do a bit of writing myself, actually...ur... would it be **O.K.** to leave this here with you?...

I'd really appreciate your comments... ...if you had time ....

Really? Ah...

..the last Tuesday of every month...usually a very nice local audience – they come to **CLAP** not **CARP**.... Getting to Rickmansworth isn't difficult...we'd just **love** you to come and talk to us...

Really? Ah.... Oh...

Can I say how much I enjoy your books!

Thank you so much! Cheers

Can I ask you something? **Why**'re you so obsessed with breasts?

Really? Ah..

It's **Phil**...remember? I was in the first year when you were ......

Oh! Ah!

... you got the date wrong..it didn't actually ..... until 1968 ... ..anyway ... ... sign this ....?

Could you put to the "Bennet Family"?

But of course!

No.1 mag for authors and authors-to-be!

YourNew Baby

Yo Ba

Yo Ba

Cruel
to be kin
When it's
ABORT y
BOOK

HOM
DELIVERY
self-publis

BOND
with your a
& your edit

YOUR QUE

• Will I ever
conceive?
• How to sto
producing
TURKEYS

5 DAN
✓ Nause
✓ Tantr
✓ Jealo
✓ Depr
✓ Cons

afte
birt

Te
w
t

Starting your
SECOND...
How long should you wait?

THE BIG
PUSH
10 PUBLICATION
DAY MUSTS

CONTRACTIONS
Things agents
daren't tell you

FACT FILE
overdue?
The danger signs

FAMOUS LABOURS
Dickens ✳ Jane Austen ✳ Flaubert ✳
G.A.Henty ✳ describe how it was for them!

FREE INSIDE! CUTOUT & KEEP CAMEOS

PLUS   Why BOTTLE is best by Ernest Hemingway ✳

best sellers....
how to produce one a year ALL your
creative life! Our step-by-step guide

PLUS   Cutting the Cord — how to switch publishers

Subscribe now!

✳

The LITERARY 3

A STRANGE PACKAGE HAS ARRIVED FOR PEGGY CHESTER, POPULAR SIXTH FORMER AT **WHYTECLIFFE SCHOOL**. HER CHEERY CHUMS, **JOY** AND **CORAL**, CROWD ROUND HER:

GOODNESS! *WHAT A QUEER PARCEL!*

YES! IT HAS NO STRING NOR SEALING WAX!

IT SAYS IT'S CALLED A "JIFFY BAG"...IT'S FROM MY UNCLE **BILL**....HE'S A **TIME TRAVELLER**, YOU KNOW — HE GOES TO THE **FUTURE** QUITE OFTEN....

DELIGHTED GASPS GREET THE CONTENTS OF THE PARCEL:

GOSH! HOW **WIZARD!** A BOOK! A STORY FOR TEENAGED GIRLS, PUBLISHED IN AMERICA IN THE YEAR **2003!** *IMAGINE!* **2003!**

"LICK MY ZIP"... MY WORD, THAT'S AN ODD TITLE!

OH DO BE A SPORT AND READ IT SOON, PEGGY! THEN WE CAN HAVE A MEETING OF OUR **SECRET SOCIETY!**

YES! THE THREE CHUMS HAVE A SECRET SOCIETY –A READING GROUP WHICH MEETS TO DEBATE LITERARY TEXTS!

HOW PEGGY'S EYES SPARKLED THE NEXT EVENING, WHEN THEY CONVENED IN DORMITORY. SIX!

SO, **TELL US** PEG! WAS IT A **RIPPING** READ?

WELL, IT'S ABSOLUTELY **"X"** CERTIFICATE! *FULL* OF SWEARING!

NO!

GOLLY!

HOW *THRILLING!*

ANY PONIES?

NO PONIES...BECAUSE **ZEE**, THE HEROINE, LIVES IN NEW YORK. I THINK SHE'S RATHER WET AND SPOILT – ALWAYS *BLUBBING* ABOUT HER PEOPLE, WHO ARE FRIGHTFULLY RICH. HER MOTHER IS A **BANKER!**

AND HER BEST CHUM IS A BULIMIC.

GOSH!

A *WHAT?*

DOES ZEE HAVE A PET? OR **HOBBIES?**

WELL, SORT OF...

..ZEE AND HER PAL, LOULOU, PLAY **TRUANT**.. THEY GO **PILFERING** IN SHOPS!

THEY SICK UP THEIR LUNCHES

THEY SMOKE **REEFERS!**

THEY GET **BLOTTO** ON BOOZE!... THEY GO TO **OPIUM DENS!**

CRIKEY!

CORKS!

AND THAT'S NOT ALL!

THEY MEET **YOUTHS**.... ..AND **GO ALL THE WAY!!**

NO!

HOW *THRILLING!*

WELL, NO, THEY DON'T FIND IT THRILLING – THAT'S WHAT'S SO **ODD**...

GOODNESS, THEY HAVE STRANGE LIVES, THE GIRLS OF THE FUTURE! SMOKING... ..SWEARING...DRINKING... .. BANGING LIKE BELT-FED MORTARS — AS UNCLE BILL WOULD SAY...

WHATEVER DO THEY DO AFTER THEY LEAVE SCHOOL??

Penny, I'm just off to *Fresherfayre* ...

16 WINTERGREENES 16

BOOKS   BOOKS

What did you say, darling?

I'm off to Fresherfayre

What do we need?

Oh....Well, we're clean out of *Jamie Oliver* and *Alan Titchmarsh* ...and *Sunshine Eating*...um...

Why don't I save *Zoë* the hassle? I can deal with this.... How many copies do we want? I'll ring the whole-saler now...

NO, Colin, ducky!! Don't even *think* of doing that!

We can get the books *far cheaper* at Fresherfayre!

I just had another idea! We might do even better buying them at *Borders*... 'cos they're doing 3 books for the price of 2 at the moment...

...and if we use *book tokens* to buy them....

Ooh, good thinking!

JMB

Let's do a little sum... Borders do 3 for 2 ...so that's a 33½% discount....

And you get 12½% off using a book token...

BOOK TOKENS

So that makes a 45% discount. And what was Fresherfayre's discount last time? 50%?

Yeah

Well, that's clear then! Off you go to Fresherfayre!

So, if they've got them: *eight* Titchmarshes...same again Jamie Oliver...might as well get some Harry Potter...and Rick Stein...oh, and while you're there, get some *milk* and some *Hobnobs*...ooh, and we're very low on *Nescaff*...um

OK

ousehold

Fresherfayre

biscuits crisps confectionery

popular title

Rick Ste

fresherfayre checkout

Persil

"Wait, Charlotte!...
You can't leave me now,
I haven't finished my novel
— I **need** your misery!"

Mum...I've got something to tell you...um, I know you'll be shocked....

I know it's against your **feminist** principles...but Ian and I, we've talked it through....

See, I've decided to abandon my book. I've packed in the reviewing, too...because I'm going to be a **FULL TIME MOTHER.** **Ian** will support me, Toby and the new baby....

Mum?

Mum! Say Something!!

Can't you spare even **FIVE** minutes from your bloody book!? **GOD!** Story of my life!!

Tell you, **I'm** going to be there for **MY** kids!! **I'm** going to be a **proper** mother!

Look, I **HEARD** you! ...I'm just thinking it through....

You want to be a full-time mother and housewife...for as long as it takes...yes?

Hmm

...hmm...that means quite often feeling **frustrated**... bored...lonely...isolated ...**marginalised**...

And then you feel **ANGRY !!** **Angry** at being financially dependent ...**furious** at being patronised....

...and, God, you'll be patronised! – **EVERYONE** thinks **stay-at-home mothering's** such a **VITAL,** marvellous job!

watch people glaze when you tell them what you do!

Enjoy the way you're treated! Like you're **brain-dead!**...

...like you're **Little Mrs Fluffy!**

Pretty soon you'd be shrieking "**Who am I?!**" and clawing the walls...

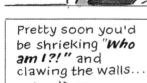

So..

...Not a bad career-move, darling..!

...there's a book in there for you! **Definitely!** Sort of book that begs to be written every decade or so... **Betty Friedan** sort of book... you'd do it brilliantly... For your generation, a **razor-edged polemic** on **Motherhood!**

THE NATIONAL CHARACTER

A Love of Poetry

Ask Doctor Derek

Doctor Derek Troutley shares his casebook

MY PATIENT, SUZIE X, WAS A YOUNG AUTHOR WITH **EVERYTHING**!.. —LOOKS, SEX APPEAL, FABULOUS FASHION WARDROBE....

...AND YET...

I'M SO STRESSED OUT... I DON'T KNOW WHAT'S THE MATTER WITH ME!

YOU SEE, I WAS **SO REGULAR**, DOCTOR! **EIGHT THOUSAND** WORDS A DAY...**EVERY DAY**!

BUT NOW I SIT IN THAT LITTLE ROOM FOR **HOURS** AND **HOURS**...

...AND **NOTHING** COMES OUT!

HMM...YOU FEEL **SLUGGISH** AT ALL? FIND YOURSELF **STRAINING**?

YES... ALL THE TIME

THEN I'M AFRAID, SUZIE... YOU HAVE WHAT WE CALL "**WRITER'S BLOCK**"....

..A VERY COMMON CONDITION... YOUR CASE IS TYPICAL—AS YOU MENTIONED, YOU'RE ON THE SECOND OF A **TWO-BOOK CONTRACT**.... AND YOU'VE TAKEN A **VERY, VERY BULKY** ADVANCE, YES?

WELL, THIS CAN WEIGH HEAVILY ON THE SYSTEM.. CAUSE IT TO **SEIZE UP**!

YOU FEEL YOU'VE BITTEN OFF MORE THAN YOU CAN CHEW, I DARE SAY....

YES, I FEEL I'M NEVER EVER GOING TO EARN MY ADVANCE!

NOW, GIVEN TIME AND RELAXATION, **WRITER'S BLOCK** OFTEN RIGHTS ITSELF...**NATURE** TAKES ITS COURSE. BUT IN SUZIE'S CASE, I HAD A HUNCH SHE NEEDED SOME PRACTICAL TREATMENT.

NOW, I'D LIKE TO LOOK AT YOUR SYNOPSIS.

JUST FIVE MINUTES' EXAMINATION REVEALED THE MAIN CAUSE OF HER BLOCKAGE: AN **OVER TWISTED** PLOT!

YOU'RE RIGHT! TOO MANY KNOTS

AND IT TOOK JUST ANOTHER TEN MINUTES TO WORK IT OUT WITH A PENCIL!

THANKS DOCTOR!

NO PROBLEM

Ask Doctor Derek

Doctor Derek Troutley shares his casebook

MY PATIENTS TELL ME **THEY** ENJOY THE WIDE RANGE OF PERIODICALS IN MY WAITING ROOM...

RECENTLY, HOWEVER, I FOUND **VICKI X**, WIFE OF SUCCESSFUL AUTHOR **GILES X**, NOT BROWSING, BUT **SOBBING** OVER ALL THE LITERARY REVIEWS....

IT'S NOT **ME** I'VE COME ABOUT, DOCTOR —IT'S **GILES**...I'M SO WORRIED ABOUT HIM! SOMETHING'S VERY WRONG, BUT HE CAN'T SEE IT!

LOOK! I'LL SHOW YOU... LOOK AT THIS PICTURE LOOK AT **GILES!** LOOK HOW BIG IT'S GROWN!

!

IT'S BEEN GROWING BIGGER AND BIGGER EVER SINCE HE WON THE **BOOKER PRIZE**... ...EVER SINCE HE WAS TRANSLATED INTO SIXTY LANGUAGES... ⸗**CHOKE**⸗

IT'S GOT SO ENORMOUS!....YET HE COMPLAINS EVERYTHING'S GOT TOO **SMALL** FOR HIM...OUR **COTTAGE**... OUR **CITROËN**...OUR **MARRIAGE!** NOW HE WANTS TO BUY A 20 ROOM **CHATEAU** IN THE TARN, SO HE CAN ENTERTAIN HIS NEW CELEBRITY FRIENDS!

HE'S FORGOTTEN HIS OLD ONES

HE DOESN'T MIX WITH **NOBODIES** ANY MORE

WHAT'S WRONG WITH HIM, DOCTOR?

HMM.. WELL..

I'M PRETTY SURE FROM WHAT YOU SAY THAT **GILES** HAS WHAT WE CALL A "**SWOLLEN HEAD**"...

TYPICALLY, THE ONSET OF THIS CONDITION FOLLOWS A PERIOD OF **SUCCESS** OR CRITICAL ACCLAIM... YOU SEE, VICKI, **SUCCESS** – EVEN A **TINY** AMOUNT– CAN CAUSE AN **ACUTE INFLATUS** OF THE **EGO!**

THE HEAD *literally* SWELLS TO AN ENORMOUS SIZE...SOMETIMES THE **FEET** DO TOO – THEY GET WHAT WE CALL "**TOO BIG FOR THEIR BOOTS** "...

HAVE **GILES'** FEET SWOLLEN?

NO.... JUST HIS HEAD.

FICTION
You, me and the Bedpost
Giles Trissper's fiction

AND IS THERE A CURE FOR **SWOLLEN HEAD**, DOCTOR?

OH, INDEED YES! USUALLY A **FALL** DOES IT...OR BECAUSE, YOU SEE, THE **EGO** IS PUFFED UP LIKE A TYRE –A SHARP PRICK IS OFTEN ENOUGH...OFTEN A **FRIEND** IS THE BEST PERSON TO DO IT...

OH LOOK THERE HE IS IN THE NEW YORK REVIEW!

Albion at
JOAN DI..

JUST LOOK AT HIS HEAD! ...POOR GILES!

Facts and Fallacies
No.6: Children's Picture Books

ANYONE CAN WRITE ONE. REALLY! IT'S AS EASY AS PIE!

A STORY TAKES ABOUT FIVE MINUTES TO WRITE. NOT MUCH LONGER — PICTURE BOOKS ARE VERY SHORT! YOU CAN DO ONE IN YOUR LUNCH HOUR...

> **There!** NOW I'll have my sarnie

NOT **EVERYONE** CAN ILLUSTRATE BUT EVERYONE KNOWS SOMEONE WHO **CAN** – WHO'D LIKE NOTHING BETTER THAN TO IMMORTALISE THE FUNNY THINGS YOUR CHILDREN SAY!
ILLUSTRATING ISN'T REALLY **WORK** – COSY HOURS AT HOME WITH PAINTS AND CRAYONS AND RADIO 4....

> It must be **tremendous FUN!**

PICTURE BOOKS ARE OFTEN WRITTEN AND ILLUSTRATED BY: (i) **WOMEN** WITH UNTIDY HAIR IN **SUFFOLK** COTTAGES....

...(ii) **MEN** WITH NEAT BEARDS, ARRAN SWEATERS AND A VIBRANT **INNER CHILD**...

> How old's yours these days?

> Oh, still about 6-8

...(iii) BY **FILTHY** CORRUPTERS OF INNOCENCE...

> I did burps, bogies and sick in the Eighties

> ...farts and turds in the nineties...

> We have to keep on pushing the boundaries!

FACT: 98% OF PEOPLE WHO WORK IN CHILDREN'S PUBLISHING ARE CALLED **EMMA** AND WEAR BLACK. LYCRA-WOOL MIX TROUSERS. AT ANY ONE TIME, **85.5%** OF THIS FIGURE ARE EDITING A BOOK ABOUT A **CAT**.

> Emma, there's a message from Emma on your desk

> O cheers, Emma!

FALLACY: ALL EDITORIAL MEETINGS ARE ATTENDED BY **RABBITS** AND A **BEAR** IN A PINNY.....

...AS ARE THE PARTIES HELD FOR AUTHORS AND ILLUSTRATORS.

> WOW! NOT **the** Peter Rabbit!

EVERYONE INVOLVED IN PICTURE BOOKS — AUTHORS, ARTISTS, EDITORS — ARE HELD IN THE VERY HIGHEST ESTEEM.

> You do a book a year!....

> ...translated into **20** languages...with **squillions** sold worldwide!?? **Why** haven't I heard of your books?!

> Well.. I write children's books

> Oh...

> And how long will you stay on the children's side?

> Oh, how lovely! What fun!

> D'you do any serious art too?

> Oh, **what fun!** Do you ever do any serious writing?

> I expect you'll want to move on to grown-up literature

Facts and Fallacies
No. 11 : Publishers' Readers

FALLACY: IT'S A CUSHY NUMBER BEING PAID TO LOUNGE ABOUT HOME, READING NOVELS.

FACT: BEING A READER AND PRONOUNCING UPON THE COUNTLESS MANUSCRIPTS SUBMITTED TO A PUBLISHING HOUSE, IS A VERY **SERIOUS** BUSINESS. A READER MUST BE CONSCIENTIOUS, ALERT, DECISIVE AND DISCRIMINATING.

FALLACY: A PUBLISHER'S READER WORKS ROUND THE CLOCK, PORING OVER **EVERY** WORD OF **EVERY** PAGE OF **EVERY** MANUSCRIPT...

FACT: *NOBODY* WORKS ROUND THE CLOCK, EXCEPT....

AT THE THIRD STROKE THE TIME SPONSORED BY ACCURIST WILL BE...

FACT: 97% OF PUBLISHERS' READERS ARE MULTI-TASKED, GRADUATE HOME-MAKERS.

FACT: EVERY YEAR A SMALL NUMBER OF MASTERPIECES LAND INADVERTANTLY IN THE REJECTION PILE AND ARE LOST TO LITERATURE. THIS IS DUE TO HALF-TERM.

MANUSCRIPTS ARE ALWAYS JUDGED ON THEIR MERIT AND **NEVER** BECAUSE THE READER CAN'T STAND YET ANOTHER **QUEST** SAGA OR ANOTHER NOVEL ABOUT THREE GENERATIONS OF MIDDLE CLASS WOMEN.

DAD! DAD! I need some money! **DAD! DAD!**

Qudok raised one finger of his mailed fist. "I seek the Sword of Durgak!...

REJECTED AUTHORS COMMONLY BELIEVE THERE IS A LONDON-BASED CABAL OF LITERARY LIONS WHO SUPPRESS COMPETITION...

Out you go!... ...you clever little bastard!

REJECTED AUTHORS ALSO WORRY THEIR MANUSCRIPTS MAY NOT HAVE BEEN **REALLY** LOOKED AT:

I think they read two paragraphs and then shove it back in the S.A.E

THIS IS A FALLACY. A READER WOULD **NEVER** PUT A MANUSCRIPT STRAIGHT BACK IN AN ENVELOPE WITHOUT, FIRST, GIVING THE PAGES A GOOD **SHAKE** — THEREBY DISLODGING THE HAIR, PLACED BY THE AUTHOR BETWEEN PAGES 18 & 19....

And the book-match between pages 258 and 259!

Ask Doctor Derek

Doctor Derek Troutley shares his casebook

GOES WITHOUT SAYING — YOU CAN'T BE **SQUEAMISH** IF YOU'RE A DOCTOR...

...BUT, EVEN SO, THINGS **CAN** SOMETIMES BE VERY TESTING......

...LIKE WHEN, FOR EXAMPLE, YOU GET A WRITER BLEEDING ALL OVER YOU....

MY PATIENT, **JAMES X**, AUTHOR OF ONE WELL RECEIVED AND BEST-SELLING BIOGRAPHY, HAD JUST HAD A SECOND BOOK PUBLISHED...

GREAT SCOTT!

WHO'S DONE THIS TO YOU!?

UHHn

≥ CHOKE ≤ THEY **ALL** DID! **ALL** THE REVIEWS...THEY **ALL** LAID INTO MY BOOK¹ ≥SOB≤...

THIS WAS THE WORST CASE OF CRITICAL MAULING I'D EVER ENCOUNTERED! **EVERY** SINGLE REVIEWER HAD STUCK THEIR KNIFE INTO HIM!

GOD..BLOOD **EVERYWHERE**

...the Guardian... and Telegraph!... **Aghh!**...they hurt worst!...uchh!..

WHAT CAN YOU DO FOR SOMEONE WHO'S LITERALLY BEEN TORN TO SHREDS?

...WILL I... WILL I EVER WRITE AGAIN, DOC?

WELL, YOU MOP THEM UP...YOU TELL THEM SOOTHING THINGS...

CRITICS ALWAYS GIVE SECOND BOOKS A HARD TIME.....ER... SUCCESS OFTEN BREEDS A SPOT OF JEALOUSY...

...YOU MENTION THE TALL POPPY SYNDROME....

YOU SEE, THE PRESS BUILDS YOU UP...AND THEN IT KNOCKS YOU DOWN. HAPPENS ALL THE TIME...

SOME WRITERS MAKE A GOOD RECOVERY AFTER A PASTING LIKE THAT...

..BUT JAMES..WELL, I'M AFRAID **HE'LL** BE BABBLING LINES FROM THOSE REVIEWS THE REST OF HIS DAYS...

"An unexpected disappointment."..
"...his research debases the genre..."
"...a marvel of ignorance and superficiality..."

SO **LISTEN!** YOU KNOW WHO YOU ARE, YOU REVIEWERS OUT THERE!... **LOOK** AT THE DAMAGE YOU DO....

THAT GUY'S BEEN SCARRED FOR **LIFE**!

...AND MY WAITING ROOM CARPET IS RUINED!

♪ aAhghh-ouuff! Thunk-bonk... Thwack!... Love thirty...

♪ aahgh-ouff! Thunk-bonk! Thwack! Love forty...

Oh, grite beck-hend returns!...he killed a lodda plaiers with those in the Frinch Open....

♪ agGhh-oufff! Thud-bonk... *Hwhhupp!!* Game to Rizla...

Ooh, grite time to brike serve!

But, two sets down, Rizla still wearing the brown trousers, wouldn't you say, Pat?...

Yih, he's godda mountain to climb, this guy...he's just godda tike the nixt gime one point at a time....

He's a confidence plaiyer...and when that's gone, he's snookered...

♪ *Ahgh-ouff!* ♪
Thud-bonk!
Fifteen love...

♪ *Ahgh-ouff! Thud-bonk! Whhup...bonk! Whhap-bonk! THWACK! Pok!*
Out!
Fifteen all

♪ *Ahgh-ouff!* ♪ *Thud-bonk! OUT!*

Hmm. Wild first service there... really errant ball toss...

click-click click!

Oh, his game's beginning to fray just that little bit, now...

Plok!

Le Déjeuner sur le Sable

DYNAGLOBE'S SUMMER PARTY... IT'S SUPPOSED TO BE A **HOT** INVITE... BUT, GOD, I CAN'T **STAND IT!** WILD HORSES 'COULDN'T DRAG ME THERE IN THE ORDINARY WAY...

I always drink too much...

...AND IT'S ALWAYS THE SAME: THAT SWEATY ATRIUM AND HUNDREDS OF SWEATY AUTHORS — ALL OF US PART OF DYNAGLOBE'S BIG, HAPPY FAMILY OF IMPRINTS...

I JUST DON'T THINK I CAN FACE IT..... I **ALWAYS** RUN INTO SOME STAR WRITER OF AIRPORT **TOSH**. [YOU KNOW THE TYPE – COVERED IN EDITORS' DROOL, EGO INFLATED BY HUGE ADVANCES, COLOSSAL SALES AND MIRAMAX BIDDING FOR HIS FILM RIGHTS]....

Who you published by, I forget?

Alsatian

WE ALWAYS HAVE THE SAME SORT OF MUTUALLY **CONDESCENDING** CONVERSATION: **HE** MAKING ME MINDFUL OF MY VERY MODEST FAME, ADVANCES, SALES AND POSITIONING IN BOOK STORES...

Mine are always **SPINE-OUT** on the shelves [if there at all]

His are always **FACE-OUT** front of shop

...WHILE **I**, IN TURN, MAKE HIM AWARE OF **MY** PUBLISHERS' OLD AND ILLUSTRIOUS BACK LIST...OF THE FACT THAT **HE** IS MERELY A **POPULAR** WRITER, WHOSE BOOKS ARE NEVER SERIOUSLY REVIEWED...

You still with old Crichton & Duff?

They treat you well?

How they doing?

O.K..they're still publishing **literature.**

IT'S SO DEPRESSING! BUT EVEN WORSE, IS THE THOUGHT OF ALL THOSE BLOODY **WOMEN** WHO ARE **ALWAYS** THERE...

OH GOD!

JUNE WHATSIT...WHO ALWAYS TRIES TO ROPE ME IN HER DISCUSSION GROUPS

Next one's **Plagiarism! DO** say YES!

CAROL? CAROLINE? I DON'T REMEMBER IT BUT, APPARENTLY WE GROPED EACH OTHER FOUR YEARS AGO...

...JANE THINGY.. WHO PEOPLE SAY I OFFENDED AT LAST YEAR'S BASH...

AND THEN THERE'S **ALWAYS** SOME IRRESISTIBLE NYMPH FROM PRODUCTION.....AND, JUST AS I START TO ENJOY THE EVENING...

...THERE'S ALWAYS THIS BLOODY COVEN OF MIDDLE-AGED NOVELISTS...

ooh!

Yeah.. he likes 'em young

Bloody party! As I said, wild horses couldn't drag me..... But I've got to go....

. People might think I haven't been invited

Nurse Tozer

Helps Dr Derek with an unexpected case

WE ALL NEED TIME OFF... AND NO ONE MORE THAN DOCTOR DEREK... HE WAS REALLY, REALLY **BUSHED**...

unh GROAN

BUT, SADLY, A DOCTOR IS NEVER **OFF-DUTY** — PEOPLE DO TEND TO PICK THINGS UP ON HOLIDAY!

EXCUSE ME...

I'M A DOCTOR...ARE YOU O.K? SOMETHING SEEMS TO HAVE DISAGREED WITH YOU...

Uhh-hh!!

GROAN.....IT'S SOMETHING I PICKED UP IN THE HOTEL.... ...FANCY FOREIGN MUCK! IT'S **AWFUL**!

THIS!? A TRANSLATION OF *Les Misérables* BY VICTOR HUGO..!

YES! IT'S TERRIBLE!.... **NOTHING LIKE** THE MUSICAL!

DR DEREK WENT PALE. SOMETHING SEEMED TO SNAP INSIDE HIM...

THAT'S NO REASON TO CALL IT *"MUCK!"*... IT'S BY **VICTOR HUGO!** —THE CENTRAL FIGURE OF THE FRENCH ROMANTIC MOVEMENT!

..THE MASTER OF FRENCH POETRY, THAT'S **WHO**, YOU **MORON**!

I **HAD** TO INTERVENE. DR DEREK WAS UTILISING SUCH **UNPROFESSIONAL** LANGUAGE. [HE WAS, OF COURSE, VERY, VERY TIRED AND STRESSED]...

...IN FACT, YOU'RE TYPICAL OF THE WHOLE MORONIC ******* CULTURE!

GASP!

I TOOK CANDACE ASIDE AND GENTLY QUESTIONED HER ABOUT HER **USUAL** READING FARE....AND, AS I GUESSED, DISCOVERED IT WAS COMPOSED ENTIRELY OF **JUNK** [FASHION, CELEBRITY GOSSIP, LOW-GRADE CHICK-LIT]...

BUT IS THAT UNHEALTHY, NURSE?

NO, NOT IN MODERATION AS PART OF A BALANCED DIET...BUT, YOU SEE, CANDY... **THAT** SORT OF FODDER IS VERY **HIGHLY PROCESSED** — ANYTHING **HARD** HAS BEEN TAKEN OUT...IT'S **PAP**!

IT'S MINCED UP INTO LITTLE SPOON-SIZED PARAGRAPHS... IT SLIDES DOWN EFFORT-LESSLY...YOUR SYSTEM NEEDS TO DO NO WORK WHATSOEVER...

...AND IT BECOMES LAZIER AND LAZIER — **THAT'S WHY** YOU CAN'T STOMACH SOMETHING **MEATY** LIKE *"Les Misérables"*.....

YES! THAT'S RIGHT... I FOUND TOO MANY **HARD** BITS.... THESE HUGE LUMPS OF TEXT! I JUST COULDN'T GET MY TEETH INTO IT!

VICTOR HUGO
Les Misér.

BY THEN, THANK GOODNESS, DR DEREK HAD CALMED DOWN A LITTLE AND WAS EVEN ABLE TO CONTRIBUTE A STATISTIC OR TWO....

...AND A STUDY OF MICE EXPOSED TO **YOU-HOO!** MAGAZINE FOUND THAT 63% OF THEIR GREY CELLS DISAPPEARED...

AH

I THINK YOU SHOULD LIE DOWN, DOCTOR

AS A NURSE, I KNEW THAT WHAT DOCTOR DEREK DESPERATELY NEEDED WAS TO REST WITH A BOOK – IT WAS **HOURS** SINCE HIS LAST READ. HE NEEDED SOMETHING **WARM**, COMFORT-ING AND NOURISHING.
LUCKILY, I'D BROUGHT AMPLE PROVISIONS...

SO... WHAT'S IT TO BE..? " THE HOBBIT,"..? " LAST EXIT TO BROOKLYN"..?

Uhh.... THINK I FANCY A BIT OF "MOBY **DICK**"!..

WRITERS' PROBLEMS
No.4 How to create a buzz

I AM THE AUTHOR OF **3** (RELATIVELY) SUCCESSFUL CRIME NOVELS.... MY PROBLEM IS: I WANT PEOPLE TO FIND **ME** AS EXCITING AS, APPARENTLY, THEY FIND MY **BOOKS**.... BUT THEY **DON'T**!

NO ONE'S INTERESTED IN ME AS A PERSONALITY

I NEVER CREATE ANY SORT OF **BUZZ**

ON THE RARE OCCASIONS WHEN I AM INTERVIEWED, MY ATTEMPTS TO SPARKLE ARE ALWAYS MET WITH GLAZED EYES AND STIFLED YAWNS.
OF COURSE, I'M THE FIRST TO ADMIT MY DAY-TO-DAY ROUTINE DOES NOT MAKE **FASCINATING** COPY...

Mostly I sit in my room and write...

Yeah?

BUT THEN, **ALL** WRITERS SIT IN ROOMS AND WRITE!!.... JUST WHAT **IS** IT THAT MAKES THE SPOTLIGHT REST ON ONE AUTHOR RATHER THAN ANOTHER? **WHY AM I** IGNORED??
IS IT BECAUSE I HAVE NOTHING TO CONFESS? — NO DIVORCES, DRUGS, FEUDS, DICES WITH DEATH? MY MARRIAGE IS HAPPY....

Yes! My childhood was very happy too!

Did you get on with your parents?

I adored them both!

I'M ALWAYS WRITTEN OFF AS A **BORE** — TRY AS I MIGHT TO MAKE MYSELF INTERESTING AND CHARISMATIC...

Ailments? Well, like Martin Amis, I've had teeth trouble... and, because my hands suffer from a mild dermatitis, I always wear a pair of **SURGICAL GLOVES** at the keyboard....

PERHAPS I SHOULD JUST ACCEPT MY **GREY PERSONA**... BUT **I CAN'T**!!
I WANT TO BE CELEBRATED!... I WANT TO TURN HEADS IN RESTAURANTS!... I WANT TO BE TALKED ABOUT!......
I WANT TO CREATE A BUZZ!

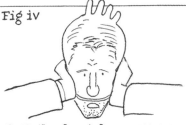

WHAT CAN I DO?

ANSWER:

Fig i

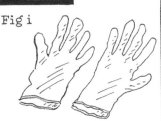

Make sure you have your surgical gloves with you at the interview....

Fig v

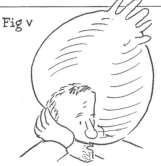

...until glove inflates to impressive size...bigger and bigger and...

Fig ii

Fig ii   Take one of the gloves and hold it at nose·level.

Fig iii

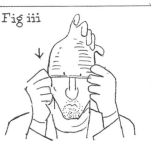

Pull and stretch the glove over your head.

Fig iv

Pull the front down over nose. Clamp hands over ears to ensure airtightness. Breathe **IN** deeply through mouth and **OUT** through nose....

Fig vi

Goodness! What a buzz!

ZZZZZVZZZZ
BLLPZZZZZ
— Blimey!

Bravo!

Encore!

Encore!

Brilliant!

DON'T TRY THIS AT HOME!

SEASONAL TRADITIONS IN THE BOOK TRADE

No. 2 Spotting the Christmas Turkeys

"...Funny, really, there were
masses of people here lunchtime, but
you never can tell, can you? I mean,
last week we had Jilly here, we were really
quite busy, but you know, you can never tell, can you..?"

MURDER AT
MATABELE MANSIONS
A Christmas Mystery

Detective Inspector Collar writes: **I**t was one of those vile days just after Christmas. Around 5 p.m. I was about to clear off home when D.S. Stoker rang. There'd been a fatality, she said, in a mansion block nearby. Accidental, according to the medics. Head injury consistent with a fall down some icy steps.

Accidental, Stoker!? **ACCIDENTAL!!?** ..Listen, don't bother me with **accidents**...

But, sir!..there's something a bit odd...

..I think you should take a look... before they remove the body....

really I do, sir

A light precipitation of snow commenced as I proceeded in the direction of Matabele Mansions.

The deceased was at the rear of the building in the vicinity of the dustbins. Beside him a plastic sack had voided some of its malodorous contents.

So...who've we got here, Stoker?

Godfrey Filbone...58...second hand book dealer. Divorced, no kids, no pets.... According to the Porter, he's a loner...

Seems he rubbed everyone up the wrong way...

..Neighbours couldn't stand him.

GODFREY FILBONE

Hmn yes...clear as effing mud, Stoker...he was bringing his rubbish down...**icy** step...went arse over tit...bashed his head..and that was it. **Curtains. Accident**...that's what it looks like

SHAMPOO ORGANIX

Kentucky Fried Chicken

kitekat TUNA

square tea bag

Round tea bag

CHICKEN TIKKA

Hmn..but on the other hand, I agree with you...**something** doesn't smell quite right about this.... ..and it's not just the **fish**

It's the **CAT FOOD!**

EXACTLY! He didn't **have** a **CAT!**

And **this!**

ORGN

Why would a **BALDY** have shampoo for greasy roots and dry tips?..**why** would he have shampoo **ANYWAY?**

PRECISELY, sir! And look in here... **Disposable nappies!** He didn't have kids! ..It's someone else's rubbish bag, isn't it?

Hmn..so are we looking at the sort of **nice bloke** who, on a **freezing** bloody night, takes a neighbour's refuse to the bins?

No sir...I don't think we are... ...I think we're looking at **SOMETHING ELSE**...

Get him off to post mortem... ...and meanwhile let's pay the neighbours a little Christmas visit.

Besides Filbone's apartment, there were ten others in that part of Matabele Mansions. Having ascertained from the porter that the occupants of nos. 46, 41, and 39 were away – winter sporting and so on – we began our enquiries in the basement, at the flat underneath the deceased. **Viv and Chris Smith-Collins** described themselves as "web-site designers". Over tea – made with bags – they said that despite their proximity to the steps where Filbone tumbled, they'd heard nothing. It was only when letting their cat in that they'd seen his feet.

In the front basement, in a stifling atmosphere, heavy with the odour of aromatic oils, was **June Tozer**, a divorcee and a masseuse. There were two cats, one hers, the other she was minding for the Boyces upstairs, as she often did when they were in Norfolk. They were lovely people, she said, sometimes she minded their smallest children for an hour or so. No trouble – the little one slept most of the time. She offered us tea (made with a bag). She said she'd been massaging clients all afternoon.

On the ground floor we paused to take a look at Filbone's flat. The door was left on the latch, which accorded with his stepping out for a couple of minutes. Inside, all was orderly. His saxophone was resting on an armchair. The pedal bin in the kitchen was empty. We rang the bell of the adjacent flat several times. The porter had told us they were away. But we saw a light under the door. In the fullness of time it was opened by **Gavin Boyce** – the Gavin Boyce, author of *The Qerak Trilogy*, *The Sword of Dorghun*, etc. Great, great stuff! I'd always wondered what he was like. We professed thirst. He offered us water. He said tea and coffee were poisons.

On the first floor we found **Denis Buttril** contemplating the remains of a Tex Mex platter, a pot of tea (leaf tea). Having drunk so much tea ourselves, I asked to use his facility. He affected not to hear me. We failed in finding out his line of business, but he said that he'd been married. No children.

Mrs Kowalski, on the ground floor, allowed us to use her bathroom. She was entertaining her daughter Maria, her son-in-law Hamish and the grandchildren. She offered us coffee. Didn't like tea. In the kitchen were two massive bones . Not her supper, she said it was the dog's. She crossed herself when I mentioned Filbone.

On third floor we rang several times. After three minutes **Tim Makepeace** (a research chemist, we'd learnt) answered through the the door. Said we couldn't come in. No way. I just had to shout my questions. Did he keep a cat? No. Did he have children? How did he make his tea? Like his mother did. Strong. Always in the pot, if I wanted to know. Always PGTips, the real thing, never the bags.

Ian MacDire, an employee of British Telecom, said he'd been watching "The Eagle has Landed" at the time we has established that the murder took place. He began a sneezing fit, and asked if we'd been near cats. He was allergic to animals. His breath smelt strongly of drink..

Finally we questioned the porter – or caretaker, whatever he was.
Then, our enquiries complete, we left the premises, pondering the strange accidental death of Godfrey Filbone.

No, I heard nothing... until the alarm was raised... I've been next door all day...with the tiler...sorting out the leaky roof

He wasn't popular, Filbone was he?

No..not a popular bunny at **ALL**

The autopsy report came the following morning. Filbone's demise had been far from accidental.

Cause of Death, sir!

Suffocation!

MURDER! I knew it!

I knew it first, Inspector!

Anyway, the estimated time of death was about 2·30 pm

Hmn...that figures..the Smith-Collins said the body wasn't out there at 2 pm, when they let the cat out

But it was there at 4·15 when they let the cat in

So, between 2·30 and 4·15. the murderer dragged the body to the rear of the building, pushed it down the steps...and added a rubbish bag to make it look like an accident – which indeed it did....

..but the killer forgot that the rubbish would provide important clues....We may not know the motive, but we're pretty sure the killer is a **TEA DRINKER**...a **CAT OWNER**...a **NAPPY CHANGER**... ...a **MEAT EATER**......and I've got a strong suspicion who it is!

Well, there we are, Stoker...just a simple process of elimination... Let's proceed at once to Matabele Mansions!

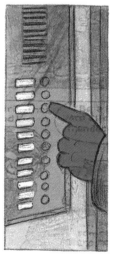

There on the threshold of Matabele Mansions we stood, my finger poised over the bell of the prime suspect.
Smith-Collins. Tozer. Boyce. Buttril. Kowalski. MacDire. Makepeace. Whose bell was I about to press, dear reader? Can you deduce, as D.S. Stoker did, the probable assassin of Godfrey Filbone?

June Tozer, the masseuse, was the killer. She used tea bags, ate meat, kept a cat, and sometimes minded the Boyces' baby – hence the nappy in the rubbish. She was also hefty enough to move Filbone's body. When questioned she broke down and confessed.

Godfrey Filbone was a client of hers, she said. He started to have a massage regularly, on Wednesdays. After a bit they got . . . well – <u>close</u>. He made promises, talked of marriage. She lent him a sizeable sum of money.

This year Tozer had planned a perfect romantic Christmas, just the two of them. But on Christmas Eve he'd rung up and said he was going somewhere else. He didn't say where. But Tozer <u>knew</u> it was with another woman. She was devastated. After Christmas, he turned up as usual for a full body massage, as if nothing had happened. He stripped off to his Y-fronts and lay down on her table. Tozer said she just saw red at this point. She gripped his neck really hard – she's very strong – and covering his head with a pillow, pressed down with her full weight. She didn't know for how long. When she realised he was dead, she panicked. She dressed him, hauled him up to the ground floor and used his door key to go into his flat. She put on one of his saxophone tapes so that people would think he was there. When it was a bit dark she dragged him out to the back door and slid him down the icy steps. She wanted it to look as though he had fallen, taking his garbage out to the bin. She took the meagre rubbish she found in Filbone's flat, and topped it up with some of her own.

Which was your big mistake!

CINDERELLA

I'm Desmond Duff, 85. Widower. Room 3, Active and Able Wing, Coffingham Court Residential Home.

I suppose if Matron hadn't gossiped about the Clissolds' party, none of the peculiar events would have happened.
("Who are the Clissolds?" I hear you ask.) They're in property. Absolute LEECHES. They own this place, Coffingham Court, where I've been incarcerated since 1998.
Anyway, Matron gossiped. And it was surprising, considering that none of us were invited to this party, how excited people got.
Even Miss Cinder – dour old bat, if ever there was one.

Enormous party they're having! At their house! It's Christmas and Mrs Clissold's fiftieth birthday combined!

200 guests! A marquee! Dancing! Sit down supper! The local M.P. is going!

Costing them over twenty five thousand pounds, apparently! IMAGINE!

25 grand!?? 25 grand on a party! ...when they spend BUGGER ALL on this hell hole!

It's a SCANDAL!!! Absolute bloody SCANDAL!

I sat down and wrote the Clissolds one of my stinkers.

...the fees here are an absolute RAMP! You bleed those of us mug enough to have saved for our old age WHITE! This place is like Colditz but you charge like Claridges! It's totally under-staffed. The food is FILTH! The hall stinks of old...
Last me...
is...

The Clissolds didn't reply. They never do. Water off a duck's back. The next time I saw them was on December 22nd, the day of their party, when they came over for the Residents Christmas Tea. Their son, Dominic, came too. And the daughter, India, who looked at us with frank disgust. And who could blame her when Mr Eggar treated us to one of his shameless outbreaks of wind. (The full repertoire of Trumps, Onion Bumbles, Cushion Creepers, Seated Cannnonade...)

♪♫ Bring me flesh and bring me wine!...

Mr and Mrs Clissold

Dominic   India

Happy Christmas! Peggy!

Joan! Happy Christmas!

Happy Christmas, Desmond!

Be a lot happier, Mrs Clissold, if you mended my radiator! ...and did something about the PONG on the landing!

Desmond, dear... We've told you before, haven't we?... If you're not happy here, you really ought to find somewhere else....

That's always Mrs Clissold's trump card. THE HELL HAG! She knows bloody well I can't afford anything better. And round here, as everyone knows, there's even worse homes than Cottingham Court.

Sherry in Miss Cinder's room only intensified my black mood. (But at least her radiator was working.) The long, dreary days of Christmas stretched endlessly ahead – no excitements, nothing to look forward to. (The poinsettia and telephone call from my son in Brisbane are not enough.) I longed suddenly for a cigarette, for warmth, love... laughter... **LIFE!**

It was most queer! I seemed to shoot up out of my chair. I found I was in my old dinner jacket. I was slim. I had my teeth. A full head of hair. Skin like a baby's! I was like I was in 1946! I was 30 again! And as for Joan Cinder!

We wafted through the door of Cottingham Court, out into the frosty night... down the hill to the Clissold's residence. And there, hungry for music, wine, love... we made our entrance.

What a stir we caused as we made for the Clissolds' booze!

And then how gay we were! How witty, how debonair, as we sipped and supped and smoked and laughed like drains! Can you imagine how it was for us to feel utterly <u>alive</u> again? . . . how it was to be released (if only till midnight) from our aching old bodies? . . . released from the geriatric world of pap-food, commodes, sticks and stair lifts . . . released, above all from the twilit corridors of Coffingham Court, where the undertakers often come and go.

Unfortunately, as the evening went on, I noticed that things had rather gone to Miss Cinder's head – I mean, what a flirt! What a goer! Whoever would've guessed it!? The fruity looks she got from all the men – in particular, from the Clissolds' son, Dominic.

When Joan left the party with that young lizard, Dominic Clissold, I was appalled!
Joan having slap and tickle! Joan behaving like Hot Patootie! And it was so damn-foolish! Had she thought what would happen to her when the clock struck midnight? Supposing she and Dominic were . . . ?
Oh, but it was too awful to think. I stood there overcome by a wave of something not unlike Jealousy.
Then I felt a hand on my shoulder.

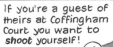

Just as the fairy goddaughter had intimated, I became my shrivelled old self once again.

But where was Joan Cinder? I began looking among the parked cars. . . .

And so we sneaked back to Coffingham Court and (after the evening's strange excitements) slept like babies. But that wasn't the end of it. Over the next few days there were more excitements, trivial in their way, but nevertheless absolute turn-ups: for a start my radiator was mended. Then the smell on the landing was dealt with. The food has improved and, to cap it all, there are rumours of some kind of official inspection. There was the sight of the Clissolds on Christmas Day. How we relished their sucking up! Mr Clissold distributing sherry, Mrs Clissold fussing and cooing . . . and the long , strange look Dominic gave Joan Cinder's remaining slipper.